Soul In Motion

Connections...
Body, Mind & Spirit

selected poems by

Rich Melcher

iUniverse, Inc.
New York Bloomington

Soul In Motion
Connections...Body, Mind & Spirit

The views expressed in this work are solely those of the author and do not necessarily reflect the views of the publisher, and the publisher hereby disclaims any responsibility for them.

iUniverse books may be ordered through booksellers or by contacting:

iUniverse
1663 Liberty Drive
Bloomington, IN 47403
www.iuniverse.com
1-800-Authors (1-800-288-4677)

Because of the dynamic nature of the Internet, any Web addresses or links contained in this book may have changed since publication and may no longer be valid.

ISBN: 978-1-4502-6177-7 (sc)
ISBN: 978-1-4502-6178-4 (ebk)

Printed in the United States of America

iUniverse rev. date: 10/26/2010

Dedication

I thank my wife, Sandra, my family and my friends for giving me good, honest feedback over the past 28 years about my poetic writings. It has been with their encouragement and support that I have found myself in that "*special poetic place*" that allows me to write freely and express myself fully.

And I would like to thank God for the countless inspirations and inner-connections that make my spiritual *and* secular writings possible.

Rich Melcher—Biography

Rich Melcher was first drawn to poetry in 1982 when—through a misty city bus window—he viewed a dilapidated athletic building on the old Minnesota State University, Mankato campus. It touched him deep within to see the similarity of this crumbling edifice to a sinking ship—with its naked flag poles, multi-level "decks", elongated railing and protruding smoke stack. He whipped out a notebook and began to describe the scene. At *that* moment he became a poet.

Over the past 28 years, Melcher's poetry has molded him into pursuing many roles, such as that of a social contemplative, a self-help encourager and an instrument for spiritual awareness.

He has a background in writing—a Bachelor of Arts in Mass Communications—and finds writing to be his most comfortable and effective way to communicate. Author of four previous books, Melcher finds that much of his fulfillment comes through expressing meaningful and educational prose and poetry to share with others.

He and his wife Sandra recently founded a communication consulting business, *Authentic Journeys (authenticjourneys.org)*, which reaches youth and adults on such topics as bipolar disorder and self-esteem. They serve the community of Milwaukee, Wisconsin with their many talents.

Eclectic Motion

s i l e   n   c   e

no sighs or violence

stillness absolute

not a breeze whispering through complaisant pine

nor gently folding lap on rocky shore

lonely hawk's absent plea cheats the cool night air

and cricket chirp choir rests voiceless

ear grasping the nothingness

       (loudest sound never heard)

to be motionless

noiseless

loud as running sap

or ant scurrying

       eardrums crying for lack of a drummer

       once *silence* is heard

       the beat

       the melody

       the rhythm

the tone

it leaves its impression forever

(the trees will know you then)

Corsair

right

in this pain, I write

in this darkness, I write

(yet, somehow, in so many ways

I'm attracted to the darkness)

in this room, I write

in this precarious state of mind

I write

where—who—what would I be

if I couldn't write?

this scribbled raw clarity inside

blind desert lost

cramped trampled thoughts and emotions

breathe free on paper

the greatest feeling

the greatest feeling

is to be a part

of something

much

bigger

than myself

something good

creative

positive

up-lifting

something involving much effort and energy

creating bonds between people and places

transforming me into an

indispensible component

calling out my abilities

exposing my talents

to be a part of bringing

life back to the lives of those beyond this skin exhilarates me

let it happen

let me play a part

a lead among many leads

Lord, give me, this day, my daily bread

my purpose

my identity

butterfly blind spot

since beginning days

butterfly has strained in vain to see its wings

velvet Picasso banners

that defy endless breeze and gust

and risk pummeling hail and deafening downpours

butterfly's inner-image being merely of a wacky

barn-storming crop duster

seemingly lost fluttering frivolously in fields of green

unaware of the gifts on its back

never realizing its beauty and simple grandeur

but merely experiencing functionality

butterfly is incomplete because it can only see

what it can <u>do</u> and not the beauty of what it <u>is</u>

not able to twist and experience the brilliance and majesty

that go far beyond flight and into a pageantry of presentation

herein lies the dilemma of *the butterfly blind spot*

think for a moment . . . . . . how many "butterflies"

have floated in and out of your life unnoticed and unsung?

never informed by you of their

magnificent spectrum banners waving proudly

while you watched and enjoyed

vaguely knowing they couldn't see them for themselves

who are <u>your</u> unkno*wing* butterflies

and what keeps you from sharing

their secrets of hidden winged glory with them?

an insight that could possibly transform them from half to whole

may I take a moment to describe your wings to you?

would you believe me if I described to you

their intricate wonders?

what lives could we change if we only took a little time

to expose the *butterfly blind spots* of those around us

and help them to become truly free?

what does it mean

in these days of hurry and often-glaring rudeness

what does it mean

to have family

to share LIFE with?

it means that no one goes hungry in the heart

no one goes thirsty from an unfed mind

no roofless tenants shiver in the soul

and no one abides in broken down shacks

of withered personality

I love being loved by the ones I love

and I love loving those I treasure so dearly

it's as though God has matched us all up

to be there for each other in ever-special ways

I see it as a poignant and fruitful notion

that it was all supposed to be this way somehow

that family is meant to be something special

and even when separated we're only a heartbeat away

isn't it amazing the feelings realigned

the time melted away

and the hope renewed like a running stream

when we get together and see eye to eye once again?

God bless the family that never forgets

the gift given in a smile, a hug, a kiss

the Presence offered and received

whenever we as family come around the bend once more

icicles

icicles

drip, drop, drip

reaching to touch

snow below

African drum rhythms pound

an ancient beat

echoing across still winter whiteness

nature-born

melt   freeze   layer   upon   layer

(life is so)

teach me, clear icicles, to take the chance

to risk non-existence

to broaden my base and lengthen my tolerance

you bleed, bleeding the only blood you know

pain of the melt brings profit of the freeze

feeling the heat and not backing away in fear

hanging in there—waiting…waiting

(if only I could do as much)

alive, as I am—if only for a short while

I admire you, icicles

satisfied in teaching me that

in comparison

I only live as long

do I choose to challenge the sun—

or rest in the shadows?

Kite string

twice this week

I've cried inside

tears warm slinking down

my sullen inner face

yet something has held me back

like being on a kite string

that's all the further

knots in the spool

the

string

pulls tight

provokes cruel wind

tension tug stress

heavy gusts of

emotion

yank

tug

-

-

-

-

snap?

-

-

-

or

bend?

-

-

-

when

-

-

will

-

-

I

-

-

be

-

-

FREE?

to prove

self

    self

        self-doubt

            the mind killer

                    been there when spinning down

                like a bug in a draining sink

                    crucifying self

                            for what end?

        to prove   worth   less   nesssss sss   ss   s

            to feel the cool squishy mud of dead bottom

                    prove?

                            prove to no one

            these are the fixings of dire depression

poet

what is it to be

poet

breeze flowing thru fingers

weeks and years of thoughts and feelings

found dancing descriptively in lines of black & white

where distilled emotion

and focused images

find home

poet

be poet

be who you truly are

far from scenes of

comparison and affirming glances

here—finding self

on the pages of the heart

poet

recognizing a soul breath

catching a butterfly then letting it fly free

exposed for all to see

yet only liberated thru catching the wind

poet

finds the simple

and creates the important

where a mere observation

becomes an entire landscape

here life comes alive

and fledgling artist

becomes

poet

Act Yo' Rage

(and I'm scared!)

as a new teacher's aide

scared of the LION inside me

"King-of-the-Jungling" all over

actin' as if he owns the place

he's just like any other animal . . . **mortal!**

and my status takes away my **tolerance . . .** my *compassion*

I fall into the trap of supremacy—like back in slave days!

me, acting out with majesty—and red-faced anger!

the violence within me starts to screeeeeeeeam

to drop peaceful convictions

to transform "from Dr. Jekyll into Mr. Hyde"

an image I abhor-------and run from!

it's me! it's me!!

I run from my own ugliness, in shame...my own evil

my own humanness—no excuses!

no reason to act as I do

it's when I no longer see the child—only flaming anger

and hatred that I fly off—

acting the same as my obviously immature students

(the worst part is) the child in me submerges like a

frightened turtle and the "me"

disappears in raging tension

(I regret it now)

being single . . . again

being human

being alone

being single, again

        no friends to distract me

      no lover to defend me

    his is the life of a madman tempered

     be it job and dreams or latte Grande

       simple special moments of solitude

     solitude up to the ear lobes and

aloneness in the presence of many talking, smiling, conversing

    folk who seem to have it all together

        the cars they drive and laughter I survive

       it's like living someone else's slippery dream

    a place setting for one in a banquet hall for the masses

      never dreamed I'd end up at this place

      only need one friend

     one good friend to turn

    this loaded, readied carrier around

  when will the winds shift?

creeping out

everything is poem

when mania creeps out

of its damp, dark, mold-covered cave

so delighted to see its own reflection

in pen & purpose

purple passion

leaks out of old wineskins

of depression and captivity

yet poem is not as important as poet

the words in volley are mere

expressions of self

not self

itself

manic trains of thought with no apparent track

wind among the smoky hills of a deeper mind

sometimes leaving engineer behind

in dust and gravel

hope lies in bending of rails

to bring the wild iron horse

back home again

to rest in the station of peace

awaiting freight of less weight

and passengers of promise

African Mask

   there is

a *never was*

this African mask I hide

deep inside me

learned long ago that the African

mask reveals

while the

Western mask *conceals*

I've worn *this* half-African/half-Western mask all my life

afraid to fully show others the true me inside,

as I goofed around, craving attention

gasping for air, waiting to be discovered

this mask of confusing shame & pain & politeness

 in the face of deadness & the hopeless

my life is a composite, a mosaic of colored

glass shards cracked off my opinions,

my ideas, my hopes and dreams

                    but now, I stand affirm and unafraid

                       to climb this greasy, splintered

ladder of identity

to a new height~

I claim my

Emancipation

freed from the deep dank death of conformity

and courteousness and polite self-deprecation

I only ask my God for one thing…Lord,

to free-up inside me

my true African Mask

so I can finally begin to live the life,

You, Jesus, dreamed

I could live

free from not speaking up when I really need to

speak my Truth

free from letting others trample my feelings and opinions

like some forgotten wheat field smothered

by frosty white winter cover

FREE to finally be **_ME_**

this is my prayer, and my affirmation, this night

thank You, Jesus!

clean page

knows more

than all

the words

i could

ever

right

battles

i

cadaver

fight

silence

is

becoming

friend

slowly

Trans form a tion

we have got a choice

a very simple choice

do we want to live a life of   imitation   and   envy

or a life of

possibility   and   opportunity?

a choice that will either launch us into new heights

of risk and struggle—hope and adventure

or dig a hole—a trench of complacency and anti-compas-
sion

encouraging a raw negativity that can squander great gifts

and crush creative endeavors

this may be the most important choice of this week

    month   year   or your life

to find freedom from fascist fruition of fateful fancies

CHOOSE LIFE

choose life

is the call

of the wandering heart

can't you hear it?

it's *possibility* and *opportunity* that cry out

to us when we seem to be falling

into the rut of blind imitation

and ugly envy

what choice will <u>you</u> make

today?

ahh

Hiroshima

let us make clean

our hands by

our

se

lv

es

//

powerful

words on a day of

anti-celebration when we

realize only a bit of what we've done

—this falling out of the sky bringing

a world of death into a new world

that can never to go back to ancient

"primitive" ways of solving

our vast problems----just

a new way of

deciding

and

com

pro

mi

zing

///

now only beyond brute strength

will solve arguments

and differences of policy and opinion

this new way of cruel quick solutions shows

worldly mega force of how ugly human beings can be

now we need a *real peace*

we need to find a solution to the solution

in time for the times ahead

seems we are approaching hell with our

military madness

can't you see it?

God, help us with an answer

Corsair, August 6, 1995

(50 years after the atom bomb destroyed Hiroshima)

the beginner

new job, new class, new direction to go

how does a mind go blank

when you don't even know

what you're doing in the first place?

this anxious feeling—it pulls and tugs on all memory

stretching it like taffy—down in a whirlpool of worry

unpredictable blushing moments when info that usually

comes out with ease is now veiled in a mist

of non-retrievable details

expectations too high and jargon too deep

like throwing the inexperienced sky diver out of the plane

and not telling 'em where the rip cord is

sad how some teach by default

then blame it on the beginner who drops wavering tray

in the lap of unpleasant past failures

coy instructors wading in their shallow expertise

commanding perfection

and obedience to the rule

yet never recognizing

that they were once

the beginner

niati

N

I

A

T

I

NIATI

NIATI

NIATI

NIATI

NIATI

NIATI

Now Is All There Is

an inspiring acronym

how simple   how true

yet these very words gnaw at a

weary soul in the laziest moments

times when *the now* is bloated with

should haves & could haves & if onlys

send the sensitive, spiritual self into hiding

to protect itself from the high, crippling waves

of inner conflict and scorching negative attitudes~

that's not the type of NOW our Savior wants us to live

the *now moment* is to be lived *just that*—moment by moment

in peace

and in love

in belief that

this NOW is

a very good place to be, and God rests--silent--in it…

as we reconfirm that Presence

now *is* all there is

whowherewhatwhywhen?

who can I be

this marvelous me

I once thought I was inside?

where did I go

this deep indigo

a darkness so rich inside?

what will I be

this suspicious me

who cancels a date on the button?

why have I come

to this city near stunned

in the waking moments of morning do?

when will I see

this marvelous me

in the eyes of my inner good self?

whowillIwhenwillIwhatwillIwho?

She went on

brush with eternity

caged by the everyday

she glanced out the window of destiny

and saw her soul threatened

when did she know that her heart was so brittle

a platform for simple sensitivities

like tender leaves sprouting in April sunshine

she had nowhere to go but the center of her being

wishful thinking and an air of good nature

singing a hopeful tune she tumbled on

there is no stopping the young at heart

even in a world divided and cold

isn't it a shame that a spirit so driven

can be captured by the small so powerful

is it not that those touched by the divine

are the most underestimated?

vicious cycles of undercurrent blues

seemed to cascade on her every limb

but she fought back with an indomitable strength

that no army could ever succumb

a brush with eternity seems to be an encounter

on the canvas of an invincible Presence

she always know her potential

they never knew what hit 'em

everybody's good for somethin'

(Arlo Guthrie)

boy is spurned for inner involvement—

    spirit bound inside

        girl entwined in gossip-ridden web that

    churns inside her, & she wonders why

        everybody's good for somethin'!

    everybody's good

     good for somethin'!

       what is this way of living

    that puts others down

for just being themselves,

    for just wanting to be found?

   everybody's good for somethin'!

    everybody's good

    good for somethin'!

it's a common feeling to be shut out of the game

to be put down, ignored & looked at with shame

we've all felt it—that lowered self-esteem

that becomes a way of being, to the extreme

everybody's good for somethin'!

everybody's good

good for somethin'!

How much did they pay

Dr. King faced dirty jail cells in the South

And death threats night and day

It took enormous patience and tolerance for him

To steadfastly follow The Way

Montgomery took the buses off the streets

And the Selma march proved to be bloody

Still, I can hear King's Grandmother saying to him

"Never forget, Martin—you ARE somebody!"

The marches and sit-ins and freedom rides

Brought Civil Rights to the fore

King led them and persuaded the masses

To let hatred be ruler no more

From the South and its deep hatred to the northern slums

He brought his cause for equal rights to the nation

But the hate & brutality he encountered in the North

Seemed even uglier than the Southern damnation

Then came his stance on a war no one wanted

But backed by a government trying to save face

I believe this is the cause that ironically got him killed

When he spoke against war in Viet Nam all over the place

It's shameful and ugly when a government hides

Its dirty dealings strewn all along the way

The only real question I have on the matter is

"How much did they pay James Earl Ray?"

much more than

recently read we are all much more than we seem

wise words that rang clear in my heart and soul

as if hearing a brand new song I've heard all my life

it is great that there is

someone out there who sees Life similar to my vision

that we are all gifted to be designers of our destiny

and coached by a Creator who brings cosmic significance

these words spoke truths

that we are

much more than

we have ever imagined ourselves to be

it is in the simple—often trivial—glance at our inner-selves

that we discover the magic of our existence, our passion ~

and what would have happened if we didn't listen

to the glance at the mysterious

or hear the scent of the unspoken textures

that often go unnoticed in the dust of daily living?

they'd be found lost in our own unknowingness

~being and knowing *we are much more*~

this is where we belong

in the mix of passionate observance

fighting distant brokenness

and hearing callings we cannot yet decipher,

but feel, none the less

here we are—who knows why—but in this <u>*here*</u> lies the fact that

the depth of our world's heart yearns to cry out

"We are <u>all</u> much more than we seem!"

oil & vinegar

           bustling   clanging

    suburban mall   food court

lotsa flashy colored plastic signs displaying

 possibly delectable entrees

   lotsa skin colors and a rainbow of cultures

        black   white   tan   beige   brown pink yellow

        yet (almost) all hanging with their own

   hundreds of people gabbing and laughing

  some (little ones) crying

              and only one mix of the races visible

        two young black guys speaking with

      three young white ladies

maybe middle schoolers--lacking inhibitions?

  this mall, this *everywhere* . . . it's like *vinegar & oil*

        thin layer connecting

           oil rising to the top—no tendency to claim

           that "I'm better, & you're not"

                          (seemingly)

but still **sep ar a tion**

obvious apartness as if wearing

opposing jerseys in a sporting event

myriad mascots avoiding one another

not unlike sides having been chosen

or borders drawn

what will it take to shake up this scene ?

blend this oil & vinegar

in the past it's taken war or athletic competition

well, we've got both right now

and still

still

still

the   mall   is   segregated

Risks

to laugh is to risk appearing the fool

to weep is to risk seeming sentimental

to reach out a helping hands to risk that hand

taking more than all you have to give

to place your ideas—your dreams—

before the crowd is to risk their loss

(or uncomfortable affirming nod)

to offer love is to risk not being loved for who you really are

to live is to risk dying—body, mind and spirit

to hope is to risk fragile fear & deep despair

but risks <u>must</u> be taken

because the greatest hazard is to keep your authentic vision

of the goodness in all

inside and risk nothing

the person who risks nothing has nothing to give

they may avoid tons of suffering

barrels of insecurity

sacks of stress

<u>and</u> the sweet chill of challenge

but may will be unable to learn

because the inexperience in failing

or dropping to their knees

will be foreign and unnatural

        chained down by certainty

        and laid low by the baggage of

        comfortable couch habitation

        they never see that only

        in the taking of risks

        can they truly be free!

this room

i walk into this room

and it's not my friend

my deadlines, unannounced

weigh on my heart

i walk into this room—my room

and i find skeletons in my closet

under my bed

creeping out and wondering

who i am today

i walk into this room

and find my naked self

bearing my trials

andiwantachange

junior higher

junior higher

Latino boy

bored with distant glance

at McDonald's Playland

little sister jumping into multi-colored plastic balls

and sliding down yellow curly-cue

too old for such foolish endeavors

too young to drive

or go to an R-rated movie

only go-carts and Disney

NO PLACE TO GO

in   be   tween

look on his face

adolescence really stinks!

reverse dandelion

imagine blowing away parachutes to the wind of a white,
fluffy "dead" dandelion
how the parachutes rest on the breeze as they expand
in distance from one another
gracefully, eventually bouncing onto green grass blades below
and disappearing from view

now envision the process in reverse
out of nowhere mini-parachutes appear
and rise into joking breeze
slowly steadily coming together in a cone shape trajectory
gracefully grouping & bouncing into one another until
they coalesce and suddenly converge on the puff-point
amazingly reattaching to the dandelion stem-pad

THIS is what God did in my life today…a grand convergence
of ample thought-soul-emotion parachutes coming back together
onto the stem launching pad of my dandelion consciousness

I thank God for this new, backwards beginning (ending)
and pray I can turn more around me into backwards motion
from tragedy and pain into bright yellow joy!

song

and the song says

we are the prisoners

of the prisoners we have taken

so often this is true

we go for so long with

NO FEAR

then suddenly find ourselves

10, 12, 20 years back

in seemingly the same position

situation

as that far-back person

"How could this happen?

Haven't I out-grown this?"

security and poise are *temporarily* shaken

but we realize it was just a glitch

and even from this, too, we can learn

(isn't that the point?)

so it's good that we see

we need to let go of the controls

and let God fly the plane

as we head calmly

reassured

to distant

destinations

Turn Around (rap)

If you come in class & you fool around

I'm tellin' you now what be comin' down

You're headin' for trouble & you're headin' there quick

And the consequences might jus' make you sick!

So what do you do? You're feelin' in a trap

We're wantin' you to change here—in a snap

You better sit down & think about it sister/brother

You need to change your tune--& soon you will discover

That the energy & effort spent foolin' around

Can be put to better uses than playin' the clown!

You gotta TURN

TURN AROUND!!

if i told you

and if i told you i was a teacher

would you believe me?

TEACHER? WHAT VALUE IS THERE IN THAT?

CORRECTING PAPERS AND TELLING KIDS TO SIT DOWN!

wait a minute   when you were 11-years-old

who did you spend more time with   your mother

or your teachers?

DON'T SIDETRACK ME! HOW MUCH MONEY DO YOU MAKE?

not much   but what are you going to leave for this world

when you are gone?   what are you going to pass on?

HEY…I'LL HAVE ALL KINDS OF $$ TO PASS ON TO MY KIDS!

AND YOU?   NOTHING!   YOU'VE GOT BRAINS –YOU COULD

BE OUT THERE MAKING REAL MONEY!

it always seems to come back to money

                                        one question

WHAT?

what did Jesus leave when He died?

JESUS?   WHAT DOES HE HAVE TO DO WITH IT?
HE WAS JUST A

teacher

and as teacher   He left Himself   He left the stories of His life
the stories that transformed lives   He gave knowledge and insight
He gave Life   He had little
money

GO AHEAD…TAKE THE GARBAGE FROM THE KIDS
TAKE THE LOW PAY   TAKE THE LONG HOURS
IF THAT'S WHAT YOU SEE AS BEING HAPPY
YOU CAN HAVE IT!!

(and if you told me i was a teacher
i would believe it?)

Enough

when I compare myself so easily

to another I think is the best

I am so often seen as a diamond in the rough

yet I am – I am enough!

times change & so does my heart

hopefully getting bigger as we go

I'm not so big and not so tough

see! I am – I am enough!

they say go out & get this—go out & get that

to be fulfilled in every way

don't fill me full of that fancy stuff

cuz I am – I am enough!

big words and action come my way

many people spout out strong heavy words

they seem to say it so off the cuff

but hey! I am – I am enough!

criticize—they criticize deep
some leave me so deflated
they try to think they're so far above
still I am – I am enough!

so I seek the positive in all I do
seek goodness at every turn
and also seek to own self-love
for I am – I am enough!

homeless ones

i share that i've never been homeless
but have come close a number of times
i surely would have met the cold lifeless streets
if others hadn't spared their nickels & dimes

i feel for the men and women in poverty
and the young girls & boys in great need
who line empty streets and dark alley ways
so many lonely hungry mouths to feed

i pray for these loving forgotten ones
and for their huge needs to be met
for God loves them in intimate connection
not a one will He ever forget!

One Family

I am Christ to you

You are Christ to me

In this body of Christ

We are all one family

We've all had our struggles

We've all been led astray

But in our dear Lord Jesus

We truly find the Way

We are all one family

In the body of Christ we find

That He has set us free

And gives us peace of mind

You are Christ to me

I am Christ to you

As a family we know

That Christ will see us through

Chorus: We are all one family

With Jesus spirituality

We are here for one another

We are all one family

(spiritual song lyrics)

attitude

they say

"it's all in your attitude"

and it's true

we ARE our attitudes

thoughts are our landscape

emotions waving wheat fields

perspective the dancing diamonds off

a cool mountain stream

attitude   so invisible

      so obvious   so indomitable

if you want to "know thyself"

just run off a print-out of your

accumulated attitudes

and your *self* will be

hard-copy evidence

p

u

integrity   bubbling

funny how a guy can go for years and years

believing one thing (or, at least, believin' he's believin')

& suddenly past images surface

disappointments, disillusionment, disagreement,

discouragement, disregard

all come

bubbling up

day turns into night (a fright, at first)

then the silent stars and yearning moon

come clear visible in the grand darkness

having patiently waited in blinding day-stream

as if a forlorn lover gazing steadily across long waters

in direction of distant mate

63

this missing love

this shipwrecked seaman

has cast his net upon me

and <u>he</u>

is

ME

his long-buried treasure—gold coins flung at my feet

is the realization of true inner longings,

once-blanketed observations

and a sturdy hull of indomitable integrity

this ME

has reclaimed the fertile soil of my unkempt

but dazzling soul

not as if a flag planted stiff on dusty lunar surface

but oak roots strong and wide-reaching

anchoring trunk transformed into an ever-widening,

multicolored upward spiral

no longer a prisoner of benign yet besieging

false fantasy friends

that for so long kept the blinders and earplugs secure

no more   no more

lie uprooted & Truth revealed

Connnnnnnnnnnnnnnnnnnnnnnnnnections

the bridge from one life

to another is the **connections** noticed

and built upon from the moment we meet another

ccccccc

    c

      c

        c

       c

         c

      connections are

        the driving force

          that attract us, pull us toward one another

           be it friendship or love relationship or

            just any old interpersonal encounter

       j

      j

     w

    w

  w

     we notice the differences, but *build* relationships

on similarities and commonalities

not superficialities, but curiosities

even the most diverse couple

can discover likenesses in *passion,*

perception and *persistence*

that bring the two as close as two atoms

t

t

b

b

b

be aware that your **connections**

with others are the umbilical cord

to your soul as you travel on

your way—they keep you on

the path, and often *create* the path

before you

to be

prove

move to

improve

never again trying to be something

for someone else

but only trying to be

to be

my best self

a true friend

funny how a true friend can be so close by

and we never even know it...

a true friend not only listens but hears...

a real friend sees beyond the glare of earthly

shadows into the essence of another...

a great friend brings out the other's best

in simple ways such as an inviting spirit

and a welcoming stance, always

making the other feel important...

a hopeful friend always has something

good to say, even when the other

is struggling and upset...

an attentive friend watches, sees, responds...

a grateful friend tells with the eyes of the
thankfulness for a bit of help or
the pleasure of one's company

thank GOD for true friends...whether a day old
togetherness or a 50-year bond...all that matters
is the give & take of sincerity, integrity and respect...

Friends are what bring life to Life!
Thanks for extending a hand toward me!

Freedom From

I've been blessed—blessed inside

with a new beginning

shackles broken in the Freedom From

Freedom From

Freedom From

a life of self-doubt

a life of thinking LACK

a life of NO life

Freedom From

Freedom From

the walls of a stifling silence

an inner-contempt that bemoans

and regrets

"that which I have not done"

and "that which I have NOT become" because of

that which I have not done

Freedom From

Freedom From

the chains of scarcity that have bound me bloody

tied me down to concrete blocks thrown

into frigid deep waters

Freedom From

Freedom From . . . now becomes

FREEDOM TO

Freedom To

Freedom To be my Best Self

in a world of my choosing

Freedom To

Freedom To

Freedom To See & be free to be my Authentic Self

and THIS ~ I promise to BE!

heart isn't in

they speak big words in strong tones

and I used to get intimidated by their eloquence

now I see that the gift I bring is that

if my heart isn't in it

I might as well not say it

it doesn't matter how I say something

with what technique or style

in favored tempo or tone

if my words have no meaning

no connection with my

authenticity—with

 my authentic

inner-self

it is this inner connection that matters most

the healthy connection to my God, my world,

my self that makes the difference between true success

and an quasi-genuine attempt to be someone else

conversion experience?

no

i haven't been converted

black to white

doubt to trust

hate to love

cold to hot

despair to joy

dark to light

cataracts cleared

i now see what

was already

there

wash   clear waters   wash

clean the mud

from my eyes

blind man cried

Jesus! Jesus! Let me SEE!!

Your faith has healed you

now I see "me"

to be poet

what does it mean to be poet?

it means no matter how much or how little

money I make

I've got a gift that no one can ever take

and that I can forever give

it means that thoughts and feelings will

find their voice in the tappings of my fingers

it means my life will have meaning because

it will be set free in capturing ideas and images

it means

I will live on paper and in indestructible

memories of those who connected with my works

it means I have a place to go, a safe haven heaven even

when all looks bleak outside, a world of life

will bubble within

it means meaning will thirst for more meaning

which will hunger for

an eternal place of un-time—and find it in forever's lap

—patiently waiting

The Motion of the Mind

cocoon

wrap me up in silk

spin me a home

to comfort

me

I

want

a warm

dark, quiet

place that exists

only to serve my needs

for life has stretched me too far

a place where I feel safe and secure

a place where I can grow and change at my own speed

silent   comfortable true self

individuality

is not a choice

it's a fact

in order to be

A PART OF

you need to be

a part from

the imitator always ends up less

because the true self is hidden

and

only in living the true self

can one be free

self-knowledge & self-discovery

seem the only ways

to find this true self ~

for integrity & wisdom

inner strengths

will shine bright in the person

who has found the self

once heard that loneliness is actually

the inability to be satisfied with the self ~

to NEED others in order to be content

yet true relationship can only happen between

those who seek to be whole

free

i remember

the joy of solid solitude

to be alive

in the air & water

swimming in a body

free from chains

or molasses stick

in the mud

fair-weather bird without feather

oh yes

i remember

the feeling of being free!

When I feel discouraged

I feel discouraged

    when I know that my job

    of which I give my heart & soul

    doesn't keep me out of the red

I feel discouraged

    when given responsibilities beyond

    my capabilities and talents

    and still they bring it on

I feel discouraged

    when my good isn't good enough

    and I worry about even showin' up

    through the doors that may bring failure

I feel discouraged

    when I have to find illness

    that'll keep me from work

    because I have fear of being overloaded

I feel discouraged

       when my spiritual life

       isn't strong enough or deep enough

       to walk thru a crucible and climb a cross

I feel discouraged…

       but I have a God who is BIG ENOUGH

       to handle my discouragement and I decide

       to follow in the steps of Christ, in the end, to the end

Whale

Anger is a whale

it stays beneath the surface then

suddenly

slides up upon a wave

and blows a spout

seeking an air it longed for for so long

even at times slapping its tail on the water

once in a long while lifting itself above the waves

crashing down on water tomb with a mighty splash

yes

Anger is a whale

and how do you control a whale?

How do you tame a mammal so free?

slanted self

in the presence of my

s

l

a

n

t

e

d

self

i see the true me

in spite of the tolerant inside

i view ugly *what-has-not-been-done*

and all the idle potential

i can feel

myself slipping into

a calm hatred

of all this that has been wasted

in my presence

in my custody

all the consuming—and little giving back

this throbbing abscess tooth just waiting to implode

and smash my self-image into shards of fun-house mirror

never to see my true image again

dangling-destiny can be a killer

all the wait on my shoulders

all the wait

desperate

words to describe my un-in-it-ness

I DON'T CARE

screams in my head

high above the city

screaming

nobody hears

nobody is meant to hear

cry hallow   but full

into the nothingness

no answer

eyes

we lock eyes

I share with you

the ME

I'm unable

to see

or maybe

the ME

I have trouble

showing to myself

or even the ME

full of passion &

playfulness

or could it be

the ME

searching for

significance

acceptance

connectedness?

but then

you free

inside

the joy

and wonder

as you

give my selves

back to

me

feel

you laugh

we laugh

that feelings are

not essential

that thinking is king

& that emotions seem to really

play little role in a healthy life

but what do people say

when they're down with the flu?

("don't feel so good")

and what does one say upon

receiving disappointing news?

tolerance

means to put up with

and not be affected

but when personal rights

are being trampled

tolerance enduring

becomes the problem

itself

Helen Keller once said "Tolerance is the

greatest gift of the human mind"

and she had a universe of struggle

every day of her life

yet to put up with our basic human rights being

trampled or ignored is to invite a world of hurt

tolerance is important

yes

to not take things personally

but when "I don't mind" is on the flag

waving above

the indifference will lead to a living death

far worse than bodily death

tolerance then becomes "I don't care"

and you've lost that battle!

listening ear

what happens in me when I sense

a listening ear? if offered by a trusted one

a spring of ideas and insights breaks forth

and begins to flow in ear direction

this can be good, that I share myself

but I must watch myself there

so I don't overdo and overextend

ear's welcome and endurance

God, please help me discern

when it is time, or not, to share

my personal stuff and inner callings

with the ones I love, and other friends

yet I know, dear Jesus, that I'm *always* welcome

to bend your ear and share whatever whenever

for this Grace I am forever thankful

and bless Your name in all ways!

lives

who would i be if i were totally consistent

what type of person would be here writing

if i didn't live separate lives

it's as if my attitudes and moods chameleon

from red to brown then green to yellow

environment has the first say

who would i be if i didn't allow my surroundings

to affect my life

would i still be living separate lives

I AM

I am who I am

what I am

where I am

because of my struggles

SUFFERING

but I don't go back

and thank those

who flung their burdens on me

I don't go back and greet

those who shut me out

and labeled me unacceptable

I don't go back and chum

with the ones who smashed

my free-flowing friendship

on the jagged rocks

of jealousy and envy

I choose only to forgive them and

thank God for giving me

the wisdom and tolerance

to keep travelin' on

despondency

in a garden of glory

with flowers and plants

wondrous and magical

all around

how could one be despondent?

old habits of thought

imprison and torture in rime untaken

& unplanned

minutes and hours tick away like sap running

and I wonder if I'm crazy for wasting time

when will I be free?

Oh, hypocrisy!

explain away

rationalize

drop deep inside

the inconsistencies and broken blindness

when anger creates a false righteousness

so sticky, so ugly

that one chooses not to look

when does one wake up

from a nervous and tumultuous sleep

that rules the moment and squashes

relationships in the fury of a calm hatred?

Oh, hypocrisy

when will you let go?

deliverance

Oh God, please release me

from the dreadful slavery of my past

  I pray You let me see the good

  in the now and let peaceful moments last

it's an emotional quandary to suffer

from deeds of days gone by

  and only see the negative, the mistakes

  & the regret in a shadowy mind's eye

I pray for deliverance, oh Lord

please part this inner Red Sea

  and let Pharaoh-thought of past defeats

  sink and drown in front of me

I thank You now for this work

You're creating deep inside

  no more to run, no more to slip and fall

  nor shamefully to duck & hide

by the lake shore

why do geese fly in a V

and scattered gulls sail singly?

why do waves atop the water roam

in never-ending direction home?

why does wind kiss flags on high

and blow dust with inaudible sigh?

why does a couple lazily walk

in tune with leisurely gate & gesturing talk?

why does light house stand tall, clean & true

while waves break at its ankles out of its view?

why does the cloud catch light like a glove

and shine forth brightly capturing sun above?

why does the loon float joyously on deep blue water

then dive & reappear in some place or another?

why do spring trees wave in steady breeze
while I do absolutely none of these?

it's the mysteries of the lake shore
and me, wonderin' if life could be more

a force of blinding darkness

who would believe that many of my deepest

spiritual experiences have come my way

 in the dreary darkness and blinding brightness

  of this traveling companion, bipolar disorder

   how could these painful blind & blinding elated times

    be God-filled, you may wonder

well,

     I guess it's all in what one considers

Spiritual

       I see the spiritual, partly, as . . .

     Whatever helps bring me closer to GOD

     Whatever helps me understand myself better

     Whatever brings me into deeper awarenesses

      of how to love others and myself

& Whatever motivates me to give others blessings given me

THIS process my illness has partaken in—

events not just handed to me

but soaking me in a rain of blessed possibilities that God has

helped transform within me into life-changing lessons~

I thank You God for this illness, that has brought

color and flavor and texture into my life

along with points of Wisdom and Grace

I never would have had

without bipolar influence

no matter the difficulties, pain and

lost-ness it has dealt me

I would never change it

even if I could—it's as much a part of me as

eye color or DNA

guess it would be like taking the tiger

out of the wild because it bites ~

this dark brilliance brings

meaning to my existence

and grace-filled gifts

into my heart and hands

to give the world

could anything be more an ally?

cloudy vision

crisp in the hollowness

all the sunken, scattered hulls of unfinished deeds

haunt me as though gravestones in my soul

as I walk in the door and back into the presence

of my responsibilities and divided attentions

they come thrashing at my throat

those unread articles and corners undusted

like wolves hungry for fresh meat

my ineptness and unresponsiveness lay waiting

still in the din of a technological encroachment

when will it rest

       when will it rest

hurricane

and so

once again

the hurricane hit the beach

(never dreamed I'd see another)

after all those I've lived thru

forecast had been sunny

vision clear and thoughts riding free

and yet the trade winds of my mind began to swirl

and high waves choking my heart came crashing in

on the beach of my soul—my personhood

lost

once again

but this time with a better shelter

than past perfect storms

do I fight against the raving

or ride it out sheltered?

(knowing that storms "don't last always")

I can feel the heat—the heat of depression!

don't run away

face your demons

but do I face them by trying to change

or understand

or let them be?

I really don't know

beyond the distressing disguise

reaching timidly toward

the mask that hides a questioning face inside~

who really lives there?

is it a *me* recognizable

or a *who* unknown, to be feared?

some never hear the silent call

to find & know the self . . .

wanting desperately

to cast down mighty shields

and shed the ancient rusty armor of mediocrity

while yearning to discard the limiting mask

and plummet the depths within

still, others find *life coach*ed

by an affirming, understanding ear that perceives

authentic greatness

behind the walls of tolerant self-dissatisfaction,

shining a warm light on a heart unnoticed—

undiscovered—

heralded—

unfolding *a way* for self to discover Self

beyond imagining

dream come true

how can I know when my dream comes true

if I don't have a specific, enduring dream?
does the leaf fallen from toppled tree

canoeing dangerously down meandering stream

know where it is going?

only knows THAT it is going

for a fantastic ride

on this river of life

no rudder

no keel

no map

no wheel

but going

all the same

believing in

having a hard time believing in

my self

who is this person

I cautiously look at in the mirror?

it's almost as if I were a foreigner in a distant land

on unfamiliar—but fertile—soil

that promises no place to rest my head

nor tend my sheep on pastures unforgiving,

with brooks babbling a forgotten tale

of who I once thought I could become

believing in

believing in

believing in myself is probably the most difficult

task I will ever encounter

especially since I seem to have

so many disparate

parts of myself all inside this one

heart, mind & soul

which ME am I to believe in and

which bloodied dream should I raise high

in this battle for pure understanding and embittering

pre-broken promises?

it is me I must believe in

but which ME and which *way*

do I choose?

tiger in my pocket

wouldn't you know

that the very pain and disillusionment I thought was long gone

rests wearily…anxiously…even comfortably…

in a beast-caging *pocket*

stitched into each garment ~ be it physical, emotional,

intellectual or spiritual ~

of my life, affecting every experience--day and night . . .

what is this creature, you wonder?

I have a tiger . . . a tiger in my pocket

imagine an old car with a malfunctioning thermostat

hot and cold unregulated—off & on, & off . . .

from frozen and too cold to start, to suddenly

bubbling over, red-lining in heat

this is bipolar disorder

there is no ditchin' it, no stowing it away in a corner cedar chest

no chaining it down in dungeon dark

one song goes, *"You can't take a lion and throw 'm in a cage and expect 'm to be thankful for the shelter that you gave . . ."*

this is the reality of *the tiger in my pocket*

it's NOT going anywhere so I better be aware that it's there

or, like a scorpion on the collar, it <u>will</u> sting

(and it may just sting anyway, no matter how aware of it I think I am)

the illness has its abrasive, unpredictable *ways*

at times like a "low-flying bomber"

dropping bombs of anger, criticism & judgment on anyone in its scope

and other times creating dungeon-thoughts and dagger-emotions

that keep me locked away in pitiful silences of screaming ugliness

yet sometimes the tiger purrs with a gaze of brilliance,

cuddly love & powerful words

...deceiver, magic-maker, genius creator...

greatest gift is to have family and friends

who have hung in there with me

from lighthouse   to ocean buoy   to life-ring   to surf board

I happen to have the <u>best</u> folk swimming at my side!

they make holding this *tiger in my pocket* livable,

fulfilling . . . even enjoyable

thoughts on loss

depression

LOSS

people

don't identify

what has caused it

supposed to "feel good"

society proclaims

when we feel bad

we think we must be abnormal

depression over being depressed

"what's been lost in my life?"

mourning death seems a legitimate result

but depression with no seeming cause?

odd commonality

depression may NOT be a waste of time

without it we may not find that broken place

that keeps us from being stuck in the past

in between

in between the black & white

are all other colors

busting out of darkness into light

which brings forearm over eye lid

darkness even in the light

sometimes I've kicked thru the door

into bright insight—even brilliance

squinting, unadjusted, frightened, buckled

in sanity and truth, bleeding &

crawling back into dusty corners

but now I choose to stand in the blinding rays

long enough for forearm to fall

and face to redden in the heat of Love's flame

letting eyes see the spectacular spectrum

of God's great goodness

which had hid in doubt

dangerously

monster in the veins

who would have known

　this amiable, peaceful guy

　could hurl daggers

　of devastating horror

　　mostly at the ones he knows and loves best

　who is this person inside a person?

　who is the monster in the veins?

blood channeled frothy & rich, in misguided

pleasantries to the brain

bashing job, place, people . . .

while dashing dreams in the rocks of

some sort of need for *FREEDOM*

freedom from what?!

(probably from his own insanity!)

unyielding　　relentless　　forceful　　focused

creatively destructive　　insightful

(all treasured skills used upside-down & inside-out)

KNOWING TO BE RIGHT

in the dusty disgust of broken-down bridges

and feelings hurt and bleeding ~

who can trust, again

the man who "comes to"

in the middle of the battle ground

seemingly *himself* again

having been this other self—this *t h i n g?*

may seem devastating and confusing to the victims

but who is the greatest victim of this "bad-blood bath"—

this brain imbalance?

the one who has been paraded around

for over a year in his body

with an on-again/off-again monster controlling the wheel

'tsbeen no fun to get little sleep and act a fool

and not know how to STOP

this roller coaster of mood, thought and behavior that

has brought so much pain and confusion

rollercoaster now stopped with meds and snooze,

maybe the monster will go back into its cave—

and with health a priority and proactive stance—

        return for never

God, only, knows...but now diligence and eagle-eye

 to symptoms must rule

to deplete and control . . . . the monster in the veins

truth about a lie

others keep encouraging me

to hide the truth about a lie

i know dagger truth

blood always springs

like a fountain

and i'm told

not even to report

be Christian

don't gossip

subtle deception

how can a lie

be healed if it's

never diagnosed disease

it goes unattended

cancerous whisper

and in denial

becomes a part of me

as i live a lie

allow it to breathe

and eventually

consuming me

The Motion of the Spirit

A SIMPLE PRAYER

GENTLE PEACE – SURROUND ME

INNER TURMOIL – RELEASE ME

HOPEFUL MIND – RENEW ME

GRACEFUL SPIRIT – FORGIVE ME

GAPING WHOLE – FILL ME

SHOT-DOWN EGO – PROTECT ME

LOVING GOD – BELIEVE IN ME

sow love

"... where there is hatred, let me sow love ..."

this

is

what I need to do—sow love!

to scatter it abundantly upon all the earth

not just on the fertile soil

but on the pathways,

the ragweed,

the thistles,

the rocky passes . . .

to shower the love given to me from God

—not so much as

to ask for or need

love in return

but to toss the seeds of love

into the whining wind

allowing the Spirit to guide their descent

to sow is to never know how my love, when shared,

will affect others . . .

never to know if they

will ever even recognize this love

only to do so . . . powerfully, open-mindedly, diligently

Spirit of God

Spirit of God, come upon us

Spirit if God, rest within us

We ask You, most holy Spirit of God,
to move among us today

To bring us solace and loving hope
To bring us friendship and goodwill
To gently bring us back to ourselves . . .

We ask this in the name
of Jesus Christ, our Lord,
Amen

prayer of a searching soul

i don't expect to *SEE*

anything, Lord, except Your Love in this world

i don't expect to *HEAR*

anything, Lord, except Your voice with me

chanting a silent beat

i don't expect to *FEEL*

anything, Lord, but the reflections

of gifts given by the Spirit

"…all I want is Your Love and Your Grace----

that's enough for me!"

oh that's a beautiful prayer

St. Ignatius—Jesuit founder—wrote so long ago

(maybe i'm meant to write prayers?)

Lord, please see me

as worthy of this prayer

an unsure searching soul

AUTHENTIC

Gratitude

God gives us opportunities

To respond to gifts given

And show appreciation

For gifts received

Through our

True fruitful

Heart-filled responses

Come our creative

Energized connections

With all around us

Authentic gratitude is our

Strongest prayer

PRAYER FOR DIRECTION

as I contemplate options

and struggle with choices

I ask, dear Lord,

that You help me keep my glasses clean

and my heart unfettered

I pray for Your Peace in my soul

as I teeter in the tangling web of daily decisions

so I can SEE and DO

Your mighty Will

And fulfill Your ultimate destiny for me

so when it comes time for me to join You in Heaven

I can look back and beyond

and know that I searched out Your path

and tried my very best to keep

my feet plodding upon it

this prayer comes from the heart

and expresses my soul's desire

so please guide me, dear Shepherd,

as I walk Your way this day

send me in a way

Oh Lord

send me in a way <u>You</u> want to send me

where to live & what to do

all up to You

this brings me—this life—

no success or fulfillment

if it is not <u>Your</u> Way, oh Lord

let Your Kingdom ride in me like

a horseman mounted tall on majestic steed

show me Your way

the Way of blessing

the Way of Truth

let me honor You and feel Your goodness

inside of me

often unaware as I am of my own beating heart

glance at me

oh Lord

as I travel dust roads

and bless my steps

as You step inside my shoes

guiding my every step

my every thought

my every *every*

Lord Jesus, help me know You

in Your leisurely struggle

to win my soul for the Kingdom

may You always rain in my heart

a thunderstorm of Faith and tolerance

as this kite of my life

battles with the high heavy weather

raw hands tugging tremendously

to keep an altitude of

Love

Thank You, Jesus, for listening to me

on this stormy night

God, Oh God

I say

God, Oh God—thank You

For the wondrous way

You've made me

It's surely a joy

To live

Live in your light

And grow in You freedom

Could it be any other way

Than Your Way in this life?

Help me to envision Your Glory

And always turn in that direction

in the breaking of the bread

how do we recognize the Presence of the Lord?

how do we sense _the terrible swift sword_?

and how do we hear him in His Holy Word?

   ~in the breaking of the bread~

we didn't see Him while walking on dusty road

and didn't recognize Him as we slowly strode

only to find Him at the table, lifting the load

   ~in the breaking of the bread~

each loaf broken into many parts

for us to handle new life--right from the start

in His presence we sense a brilliant work of art

   ~in the breaking of the bread~

Jesus becomes visible in the preparation

not to leave us in doubt, hatred and separation

but loving us in each & every situation

   ~in the breaking of the bread~

when it becomes real to us all

we come together as one, in The Call

no longer to feel frail or weak or small

~in the breaking of the bread~

we proclaim "He is risen indeed!"

for Him to meet every dashed and forgotten need

and moving us, in Grace, with Him in the lead

~in the breaking of the bread~

Grace handed to us by one another

by every person—whether sister, friend or brother

in glory, honor & praise--there is no other

~in the breaking of the bread~

we call Jesus Lord—we call Him friend

He sees us struggle, yet sees us through to the end

by giving us the Grace to heal and time to mend

~in the breaking of the bread~

What can Jesus do?

In times of trouble and strife

When my head bends down in sorrow

I want to know what is the truth

So, what can Jesus do?

I've tried my best

To follow the way shown me

And still my struggles don't pay off

But what can Jesus do?

I believe in the Lord

And the Word He has set out

But stumble to find the right words tonight

Hey!   What can Jesus do?

Truth is...he can make

All my dreams come true

If I'm patient with the process

And hopeful in the outcomes

Our Jesus is the Magnificent One
Who knows the way for me
Better than I could ever imagine
And He's on my side all the way!

So it's time to let my Faith be free
And know that my pain has not been in vain
For I know exactly what Jesus can do
He can make me who I was meant to be
(and that is "great")

THAT is what Jesus can do!!

too hard

trying too hard

to seek a sign

from on high

can distract

one from

true signs

of the Spirit

yearning for

inner-guided

movements

whispered

wisdom

un-heard

but known

to force

some type

of outer

acknowledgement

         may keep

   the real

truth

within

    unspoken

       dormant

utterances

actually believing that God is <u>within</u> us

such dangerous talk

but 1 Peter 4:11 reads

"...whoever speaks is to do so as one who is speaking

the utterances of God..."

takes a heck of a lot of spiritual confidence

to live this way, don't you think?

(the reading continues)

"...whoever serves is to do so as one who is serving

by the strength which God supplies..."

serving

Jesus was (is) THE *servant-leader*

and the strength which God supplies

is the very strength that our Lord offers us

each day, in so many ways

this in-dwelling Christ who lives in and through us

in our actions, in our example, in our Christian walk

(1 Peter ends with…)

"…so that in all things God may be glorified through Jesus Christ

to whom belongs the glory and dominion forever and ever, Amen."

it's the *in all things* that seems most challenging all things . . .

like our suffering, doubt, confusion, anger,…even disbelief?

but it says ALL THINGS . . .you mean, God can take in

and make holy and acceptable the very things we are ashamed of,

struggle with and even fail in?

(WOW! God is bigger and more loving than I thought!)

maybe it's through understanding—then believing in—God's Word

that we can BE Jesus, in our ordinary, every-day lives?

no, we need not cure lepers, give vision to the blind or feed the
5,000

but to "cure" and "bring sight" and "feed" with the gifts

we've been given (if we'd only recognize them

and their healing, assuring power) hen we WOULD BE

bringing glory to God in a simple, yet magical way!

Lord, thanks for the inspiration

and for helping us <u>live</u> <u>out</u> Your *utterances*!

a disciple's prayer

I pray today

that my gifts become gifts to you;

that my joys bring out your joys;

that my burdens-expressed become

your burdens-eased...and your

burdens-expressed may bring you ample peace;

that the vision of our Lord

that I've been given help define

the vision you see and live out.

In all ways,

may peace be with you,

always.

Amen

the canvas of my heart

be my canvas, oh spirit of Truth

to guide me ever on my way

there to enlighten and to soothe

my journey throughout the day

a canvas of Hope, a canvas of Peace

You guide me at every turn

my pain and sorrow to release

old memories no longer to burn

be my canvas, oh Lord, in every way

readying a place for paint to rest

in a multi-colored majesty

as I give the world my best

letting go of outcomes and selfish desires

You bless me with a fresh place to paint

Your canvas, clean & white, inspires

the blessings fit for a saint

be my canvas, oh spirit of Love

to guide this shepherd's path

send me gracious blessings from above

and bless my weathered shepherd's staff

help me mold this staff into a brush

to paint Your Will in colors wild & free

so as to adorn Your canvas in a silent hush

and I become the painter You want me to be

lost soul

sometimes I feel so lost

like a skimpy raft set out to sea

        abandoned

               reckless

      cast-away

it's as if my soul is crying out

for some form of significance

or signal that it's worthy

& worth something more

than just a flat breeze

on a rainy day

it's as if my heart never

developed

      and my mind brings

back only the negative

destructive memories—

never remembering the freedom

the love

the comfort

of so many pleasant passed moments

why does my mind do this?

I don't get it

on the wave-washed raft of

a lost soul

tested by fire

Lord, oh Lord, raise me higher

may I not be tested by fire

tested by water—

   You keep me from drowning

tested by wind—

   the trees sway surrounding

but give me the Grace

  to live well in this place

   & may I not be tested by fire

Refrain: tested by fire, tested by fire,

    may I not be tested by fire

when my vision's a blur

  and my mind confused

   You see me and act before

    all my patience is used

(Refrain)

when I'm suffering too much

You drive evil away

You bless me by night

and protect me by day

(Refrain)

You give me a way

to see Your truth again

I give You my heart

and I gain a best friend

(Refrain)

Lord, please give me the Grace

to live well in this place

and may I not be tested by fire

grateful

Oh Lord,

    may that I be grateful~

    it was in Your gratitude that the twelve

    were blessed, and how the two walking to

    Emmaus recognized Your Presence

in the breaking of the bread

    it was gratitude

    that brought me to You

    as my main man

    my true God

    my best friend and confidante

You showed me how to be thankful for the little things

    necessities of food, shelter, health, well-being,

    relationships and work

    to keep me satisfied and occupied

    I thank You for my life

my friends, my family ~

it is through You and in You

that I have my being

Glory to You, always!

religion

    expected

        unchosen

            makes

                false faith

                    protected

                    frozen

                  stiff

          dead

possible

Mark 9: 23 . . . "everything is possible

for him who believes"

is it possible

that all it takes

is for you to believe

and it will be?

the power of belief

makes it possible for dreams

to become realities

even in places once thought

impossible and impassable

but the bridge appears

and the crossing occurs

when you choose to believe

in the impossible

as if it were truth

un-done for, un-done in & done by

God makes a way of no way

a place in no place

a time in no time

and grace from disgrace

this is a God who loves us

into being

and hopes us

into loving

and make the possible

from this impossible

this is God's WAY

Grati

In this moment

I choose to love

In this moment

I choose to see

In this moment

I choose to feel

And from love

I see the truth

And feel the depth

Of my gratitude

For all gifts given ~

Thank You God for

This whispering wind

thru ancient pine

On a cool summer's day

humble prayer to my Highest Power

Dear God in Heaven,

Holy is Your Touch and Your name!

Please show me Your WAY—in front of me and inside me.

Bring me the awareness of how to be good and holy here on Earth,

my home, as I make my way in the direction of Your home, Heaven.

Please feed my hunger, quench my thirst and touch my heart,

as You provide the same for ALL Your children.

I ask You to forgive me for the times I have hurt others(and myself),

just as You instruct me to forgive others who have harmed me.

May I do so with Your Grace and Your Love.

Please put me on the right path, donning a blessed perspective,

and keep a bright light above this path so I can find the way.

Lead me through trouble spots and protect me from the evil one, *in all the forms in which these evils exist.*

I know You have the power to bring me through,
and that You will enlighten and strengthen me in Your Way—
as I strive to exemplify Your Kingdom-ness—
in all that I think, feel, say and do.

I Love You, and long for Your Presence—visible in my life
and invisible in the gift of my treasured clean heart.
Please help me bring that Presence to all I encounter,
each and every day of my life!

Lovingly,
Your servant, Your struggler,
Your student, Your admirer.

<u>here I am, Lord . . . right here, right now</u>

when have I come to You

and You were not there?

yet, when have I seen Your light

and chosen not to be warmed by it?

and when have You touched me, held me in Your arms,

blessed me in my heart, reached for me in my loneliness,

sent loved-ones to be at my side,

and made me known to You—as You watched me grow?

yet, Lord, when have You called to me, sent for me,

whispered in my ear, and I was too full of myself

to find humility and seek out Your voice?

when will I learn that You know me so well and rest

so deep within me that I cannot steal away from

Your challenge of living Your *example*?

oh, how I want to be there for You,

as You are always here for me,

in me, behind me, ahead of me, beside me all the way

it was once expressed—

Lift me, Lord, above my narrow horizons,

so I may see Your true vision for me!

so, in that spirit, please help me live a life of earnest prayer,

praising You in the triumphs <u>and</u> the struggles

as You bring my often-mundane life

alive with Your radiant Presence!

this I ask of You, Lord, right here—right now . . .

not worthy

strange feelings at times

just felt a tinge of "I'm not worthy"

roll through my heart & mind

simply because I had someone do me

a big favor--it's people helpin' people, you know

not worthy

cause I'm a sinner

and my God is perfect

how can I even claim God's goodness

when I fall down in so many ways?

not worthy

when I am so judgmental of others

and seem to value them for what they

have to give to me

I'm not worthy

but God grandfathers me in

to His Presence in time

in time

out of time

When souls meet

God

Dances

<u>pray</u>

I've had someone prayin' for me

I know it's true

you've been reaching out in prayer for me

yes, I know it's you

...I pray for you...

but you see it goes both ways

'cause you've been lifted up by Christ too

through the prayers of my heart and soul

by the handy-craft of this spiritual tool

...you pray for me...

and the differences have been remarkable

even as life strife seems to tumble on

but it seems I'm not bothered by it anymore

the Spirit has come and the Spirit has won

...and watch God change things...

once thought atop that lonely mountain peak
alone I cried and alone I stood
but I now know, with your help, Christ is <u>in</u> me
all the time—GOD IS GOOD!

Oh Holy One

We come before You in praise and thankfulness

for the countless blessings bestowed upon us.

It is our privilege to call You Lord...it is our privilege

to be graced by You.

What can we give back to repay you for

these great works in our lives?

If it were gold, may You be adorned with rooms-full

of the finest precious metals;

if it be food and drink, may the grandest banquet

be laid out before You; if it be vestments,

may the most elaborate tailored-ware

be put before You.

But these be mere earthly treasures, ones that we may

seek here today,

yet they mean nothing

to You in your Spiritual Omnipresence.

I would imagine that what you really desire from us

is a kind word in our impatience,

a good deed in our busy-ness,

or an act of Love in a moment of intolerance.

You are the King of the simple!

It only takes a second to offer up a prayer

for a loved-one in need;

it only takes a moment's thought to remember to

buy a card for a grieving friend;

it only takes a minor gesture to hold open the door

for the one coming behind

or to smile at a child coming our way.

We pray that we can be open to the possibilities of serving You

and in doing so, we offer these gifts of service to You

in hopes that we be worthy of Your graces. For it is in YOU

that we find our hope, in YOU that we experience strength,

and in YOU that we have been taught how to truly Love,

and live lives of humble gratitude.

May we always find ways to express this Love,

no matter our mood or circumstances.

We ask for Your Grace and Presence always, Amen

gentle spirit

gentle spirit

    come to me~

        gentle spirit

            help me see~

      of all the multitudes

           you chose me

          gentle spirit

      come to me

the call of St. Francis

called

had it all together

when he heard the call

listen to the trees

and the night whisper

their heights and valleys

from the depth of shallow streams

what he heard

make me an instrument of Your Peace

echoing off the hillsides of Assisi

while he thought time may have been unkind

and yet his longings of hope and love still lingered

slowly

feverishly

this call

heard many times before

in the creatures he'd befriended

this time somehow different

more peaceful

God knew it was

The Way

The Truth &

The Life

and God laughed in recognition and delight

for here was a chance

for the beginning of the middle to end

God waited

Francis responded

(and the world breathed deep)

Present

when we're here

THERE

seems so tantalizing

when we've got free time

wasted time is so coveted

absentee motivation seems to be the reality

wanting to be there   when we're here

lack if ability to live in the present

always wishing for

and never reeling in

what we're hoping and pleading for

then not wanting what we got when we get it

so, we can say a little prayer:

"God, please help me be who I am

how I am,

where I am,

when I am . . .

help me be truly present today!"

the Fountain of YOU

You, God, are the fountain of my soul

this water that streams so high and free

belongs to You

even though most others see it as

<u>my</u> gifts, <u>my</u> talents, <u>my</u> expression

yet now I know

You're not only the fountain

but the water itself!

and me?

simply the form, the height, the force

that Your Spirit sends me

up & down & through & up & out again

what a blessing—what a gift of humility—to see

*that You are the very **essence** of my being*

and as I grasp and realize that I once thought

I was that water—or even the fountain . . . ?

sometimes humility comes only through the recognition

of our insignificance . . . which then points

to our precious indispensability

no accidents

Faith calls us to see that

   there are no accidents—just God-incidents

      tested by Rwanda and the Sudan

         with crippling violence and slaughter

            how could there be "no accidents"?

I guess it occurs in how we deal with what happens to us

one sage said, "it's not what happens to you

      it's what you do with what happens to you"

     and the God-incidents arise like the phoenix

    in the choices we make, the decisions we follow thru on

   that lead to growth, wholeness, health

  and a loving response

fruitless gain

tried to lift a foot unguided

tried to bend a knee to wrong source

tried to see a way through ugly walls

it broke me like a branch, of course

I moved to know the unknowable

and have what could not be owned

knew not what I was doing when

I threw down the wrong seeds to be sown

spent time with a banished fear

spent dime upon dime on hate

lost my soul for a time so long

that I thought heaven would never wait

but somehow a light shown through at last

and Jesus came to me anyway

He chose to spare my heart, mind and soul

rescuing one who had been led astray

and since He saved me in a flash
I have a new forceful attitude
now I know my surest prayer
is humble heart-felt gratitude

Jesus Prayer

Lord Jesus Christ,

I come to You in this time of joy

knowing I've had many times of sorrow

also knowing that You were with me then

as You are with me now

it's such a blessing to realize You are my Lord and Savior

and died for me and for all with such courage and Love

for you ARE the Son of God, the most High

who rose from the dead to free us all

Hallelujah Jesus

I praise Your name!

greatness flows and goodness grows

from all You did then and all You do now

what a marvelous example You've given us

to live our lives in the fullness of Your Word

I honor You not only for what You've done for me

but for the countless ways You've loved us all

offering Your Presence and Your Grace

at times of need and lack

and times of joy and happiness

and everywhere in between

Hallelujah, You have risen indeed!

shall be retained

. . . whose offenses you forgive shall be forgiven

and whose offenses you retain shall be retained . . .

then I suddenly saw myself in the mirror

resentments, jealousies, self-hatreds galore

all the ugliness of my soul came pouring out

a spigot turned on full had begun spilling onto the floor

"Now I see where my anger was coming from!"

the answer had been revealed in one word..."retained"

so often I have held onto my resentments

as if hugging a snuggly teddy bear

grasping hold to never give them up

for the strange comfort they provided me there

retained

the petty jealousies I've embroiled in my fear-laden heart

like a flaming burger on a summertime grill

bursting with the juices of regret and lost pride

for my not having climbed a similar hill

retained

and the menacing self-pity entrenched in my psyche

that has smoldered for so many years isn't working

in the back of my sullen smoke house mind

that's provided me with its savored meat of *grief lurking*

retained

I know and see the ruins that my retention has created

and God now calls to my humbled heart born anew

to turn "retained" into a healthy "letting go"

and find new ways of allowing love to flow from me to you

Spiritual walk

the rocks, breeze & trees talk
on my daily spiritual walk
I come to see new vistas
of a world never imagined
and enter the lives of loved ones
thru a walk with Mary
and the Mysteries of a deeper life

reset and refocused I walk my way
into a more abundant world
where Jesus' miraculous past merges
with present realities
creating a hopeful, tranquil Presence
God-bonded & spirit-spoken

Clean Heart

only with a clean heart, Lord Jesus
can I truly serve Thee
only with a clean heart, Dear God,
can I truly worship Thee
only with a clean heart, Gracious Spirit
can I fully follow Thee

why do I end up with a bruised and broken heart
when the trials of life come crashing in?
would there be a way that Your Baptism water
could cleanse my heart from my every sin?

I need a cleansing flow of Your life-giving water
to make this and every day worth living
so feed my roots and prune my branches
build in me a life of not taking but giving

please give me a clean heart, Dear God
and take my deaf and blindness away
so I can see and love and serve you forever
and love all whom I meet on the way....Amen

Lord, please

Lord,

    please quiet my mind volume

    heart race

    soul voices

    body ten-shun

Lord,

    please bless me forwards

    bless me backwards

    bless me sideways

    bless me all ways

Amen

faith being forged

faith

 hot iron tested

 orange glowing

 pounded out

 by my Spiritual Blacksmith

 my questions

 my doubts

 my will to truly understand

 and fully believe

 valued

 in a process so personal

 so substantial

 so simple as

 prayer

 from quiet longing

 to silent acceptance

 God respects my process

of slowly being transformed from

boiling molten iron

to long red-hot bands of steel

then to useable, approachable,

palatable products

only created through the

furnace-driven ways of

faith being forged

Gratitude

sun setting in cool April sky
but for the Grace of God go I
a day gone by and I hadn't thought
or noticed gifts given I had not sought

it hit me hard to serve a meal
to the disadvantaged, the poor—for real
and in their faces I saw myself
my hidden ghost upon a shelf

but when I closed the door to leave
God said to me "Do you not believe
these very people you served today
could have been you, or could be you someday?"

my throat tightened with a throbbing heart
as I realized I'd forgotten the most important part
of my faith, religion and spirituality
it is <u>gratitude</u> that needs to be most important to me

for it is God's Almighty plea
for us to know and come and see

that thankfulness is a grand virtue
as faith and hope and love are too

as I drove away in awe of God's Grace
with a simple message and a smile on my face
"to say 'thanks' as often as I say 'please'
and to see Him in the least of these"

'Our Father' (de-mystified)

Dear God in Heaven,

holy is Your Presence and Your name!

   Show us Your Kingdom—

      in front of us and inside us,

         and let us know Your idea of good

            here on Earth, like it is in Heaven.

Please feed our hunger and quench our thirst today,

   and forgive us for the times we have hurt others,

      just as we forgive others who have harmed us.

Put us on the right path and keep a light above it

   so we can find our way~

      lead us through trouble spots

         and keep us covered from the evil one,

            in all the forms in which he hides.

We know Your Kingdom has the power

to bring us through

and that You are the Glorious One,

now and always!

on the way to the cross

when the bully dug a trench for me to bury my dignity alive

You filled it with Your Love and helped me to survive

~ it happened on the way to the cross ~

then the teaser spoke words of hurt and untruths

about my character

You came upon the scene to displace the slanted detractor

~ all on the way to the cross ~

a push and shove came my way to disturb my peace

you steadied my mind and cooled my temper 'til anger ceased

~coming to me on the way to the cross ~

when crushing anxieties filled my heart and mind with pain

You gave me a glance of You at the rock

that fateful night, once again

~ blessing me on the way to the cross ~

and when I rise above troubles and Your Resurrection

I clearly see—I know <u>You</u> <u>knew</u> this was Your ultimate destiny

~ as You toiled on the way to the cross ~

so how do I meet my daily trials and pains?

I recognize You on every step of the way

Rising above with joy as I say,

"I found You, on the way <u>through</u> my cross!"

Amen

pathways chosen

pathways

chosen

from here to there

maybe back again

and I am thankful for a loving God

who sends me—encouraging me

providing warm light at the end of the tunnel

so I may continue to grow

beyond my present limits

while aware of healthy boundaries

oh how wonderful it is

to be on the path

way on down the long country road

in search of my best self

seeking the authentic life

some call it *soul searching*

(I think it's much more)

to be aware of the true self

watching, listening, feeling, touching, whispering

is to know the soul

and how important it is to observe and also breathe in

the words, actions, feelings, perspective, unspokens of others

and encourage them to discover their best selves

on a blessed mission

purposeful

mindful

I call this *creatively building souls*

a venture wide and deep

we never know, really, how we will influence others

but isn't it a good policy to try beyond trying

to uplift and uphold rather than detract and scold?

many are the choices we hold in our palms~

will *your* hands bring a blessing

or deflection of love's fervor?

the question is ours to ponder and plan

as we travel down our pathways chosen